D1606915

COUNTRY PROFILES

FINLAND

BY ALICIA Z. KLEPEIS

BELLWETHER MEDIA • MINNEAPOLIS, MN

Blastoff! Discovery launches a new mission: reading to learn. Filled with facts and features, each book offers you an exciting new world to explore!

BLASTOFF! UNIVERSE

BLASTOFF! Beginners

GRADE K

BLASTOFF! READERS

GRADES 1-3

BLASTOFF! DISCOVERY

GRADE 4

This edition first published in 2023 by Bellwether Media, Inc.

No part of this publication may be reproduced in whole or in part without written permission of the publisher.
For information regarding permission, write to Bellwether Media, Inc.,
Attention: Permissions Department,
6012 Blue Circle Drive, Minnetonka, MN 55343.

Library of Congress Cataloging-in-Publication Data

Names: Klepeis, Alicia, 1971- author.
Title: Finland / by Alicia Z. Klepeis.
Description: Minneapolis, MN : Bellwether Media, Inc., 2023. |
    Series: Blastoff! Discovery : country profiles | Includes
    bibliographical references and index. | Audience: Ages 7-13 |
    Audience: Grades 4-6 | Summary: "Engaging images accompany
    information about Finland. The combination of high-interest subject
    matter and narrative text is intended for students in grades 3
    through 8"– Provided by publisher.
Identifiers: LCCN 2022050048 (print) | LCCN 2022050049
    (ebook) | ISBN 9798886871470 (library binding) | ISBN
    9798886872736 (ebook)
Subjects: LCSH: Finland–Social life and customs–Juvenile literature.
Classification: LCC DL1012 .K64 2023 (print) | LCC DL1012
    (ebook) | DDC 948.9704–dc23/eng/20221018
LC record available at https://lccn.loc.gov/2022050048
LC ebook record available at https://lccn.loc.gov/2022050049

Editor: Rachael Barnes   Designer: Brittany McIntosh

Printed in the United States of America, North Mankato, MN.

TABLE OF CONTENTS

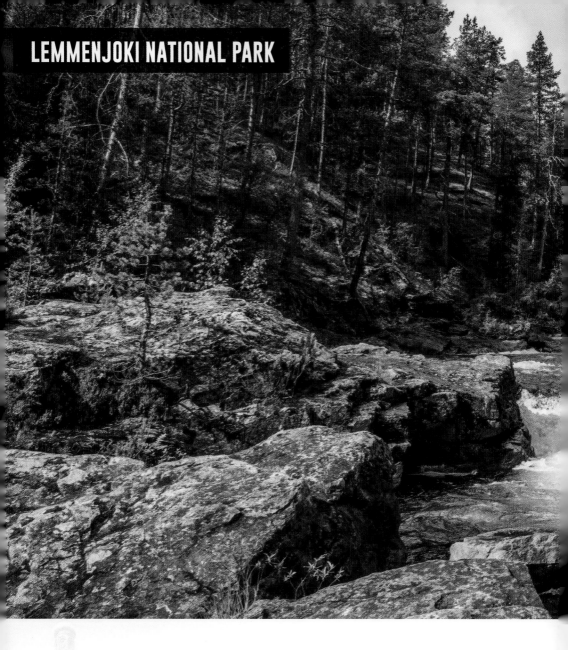

LEMMENJOKI NATIONAL PARK

A group of campers crush pine needles under their feet. They are hiking along on a forested trail in Lemmenjoki National Park. Siberian jays whistle and chatter as they fly overhead. Eventually, the campers reach the Lemmenjoki River. They take out foldable rods from their packs and spend the afternoon fishing.

OTHER TOP SITES

LAKE SAIMAA

OLAVINLINNA CASTLE

SALLA NATIONAL PARK

USPENSKI CATHEDRAL

After catching some pike and trout, they head back to their campsite. They cook their fish over a fire. In the distance, a wolf howls. The autumn air gets chilly as the evening unfolds. Just before bed, the **northern lights** turn the sky into a blanket of blues and greens. Welcome to Finland!

5

Finland is a **Nordic** nation in northern Europe. The country covers an area of 130,559 square miles (338,145 square kilometers). Northern Finland lies above the **Arctic Circle**. The capital city, Helsinki, is in the far south.

Sweden is Finland's western neighbor. Norway lies to the north. Forests form much of the long eastern border with Russia. Parts of the Baltic Sea surround much of Finland. Waters from the **Gulf** of Finland lap the nation's southern coast. Waves from the Gulf of Bothnia wash onto Finland's southwestern shores.

NORWAY

SWEDEN

THE ÅLAND ISLANDS

Over 6,700 islands make up the territory of Åland, located off Finland's southwest coast. People live on only about 60 of these islands. They speak Swedish and have their own government.

ARCTIC CIRCLE

RUSSIA

FINLAND

TAMPERE

GULF OF
BOTHNIA

TURKU   HELSINKI
        ESPOO

ÅLAND
ISLANDS
                              GULF OF
                              FINLAND

BALTIC
SEA

LANDSCAPE AND CLIMATE

Lowlands make up most of the landscape in Finland. However, several steep peaks of the Scandinavian Mountains stand out in the northwest. Forests blanket central and southern Finland. Pine and spruce trees make up many of these forests. **Deciduous trees** like birch and aspen are found in the south.

LAKE SAIMAA

= SCANDINAVIAN MOUNTAINS

LOTS OF LAKES

Finland's nickname is "the land of a thousand lakes." But the country actually has around 188,000 of them! Lake Saimaa, located in eastern Finland, is the nation's biggest.

LAKE SAIMAA

HELSINKI

Average
seasonal highs
and lows

JANUARY
HIGH: 30 °F (-1 °C)
LOW: 21 °F (-6 °C)

APRIL
HIGH: 47 °F (8 °C)
LOW: 33 °F (1 °C)

JULY
HIGH: 72 °F (22 °C)
LOW: 57 °F (14 °C)

OCTOBER
HIGH: 48 °F (9 °C)
LOW: 38 °F (3 °C)

°F = degrees Fahrenheit
°C = degrees Celsius

All of Finland has short summers and long, cold winters. The Baltic Sea keeps southern Finland more mild. But temperatures are much colder north of the Arctic Circle. During winter, the sun does not rise for over 50 days in this area. This is known as polar night.

9

Arctic terns soar over Finland's coasts. They plunge down to catch fish near the water's surface. Pike and perch swim in the many lakes scattered throughout the country. Wolverines roam widely in search of food. They **scavenge** for the meat of animals like moose.

In the forests, great gray owls feed lemmings to their young. Lynxes move quietly through the trees. They sneak up on their prey. Brown bears wander, though they are rarely seen. Reindeer **graze** on lichen and berries. They live in herds in forests and on the northern **tundra**.

REINDEER

GREAT GRAY OWL

MOOR FROG

EURASIAN LYNX

COLOR CHANGERS

Moor frogs are some of the few frogs that call Finland home. They are usually brown. But male frogs turn bright blue for a few days to find a mate.

WOLVERINE

WOLVERINE

Life Span: up to 13 years
Red List Status: least concern

wolverine range = ▮

LEAST CONCERN	NEAR THREATENED	VULNERABLE	ENDANGERED	CRITICALLY ENDANGERED	EXTINCT IN THE WILD	EXTINCT
▲						

Finland is home to over 5 million people. More than 9 out of 10 are Finnish. The second largest group of people are Swedish. Smaller groups of Russians, Estonians, and Romani people dwell in Finland. The Sámi are **Indigenous** people who call northern Finland home. Their **ancestors** have lived in the area for thousands of years.

Roughly two out of three Finns are Lutheran. It is a form of Christianity. But many other Finns follow no religion. Both Finnish and Swedish are official languages. However, far more people speak Finnish. Many Finns also speak English.

FAMOUS FACE

Name: **Tuukka Rask**
Birthday: **March 10, 1987**
Hometown: **Savonlinna, Finland**
Famous for: **A professional hockey player in the National Hockey League who played on multiple All-Star Teams and is the all-time wins leader in Boston Bruins history**

SPEAK FINNISH

ENGLISH	FINNISH	HOW TO SAY IT
hello	hei	hey
goodbye	näkemiin	KNACK-eh-meen
please	olkaa hyvä	OAL-kah WHO-vah
thank you	kiitos	KEE-tohss
yes	kyllä	KOO-lah
no	ei	AY

LAPPEENRANTA

SUMMER COTTAGES

It is common for Finns to own a summer cottage, or *mökki*. Many are located near a lake or by the ocean. These vary in style from simple wooden huts to much fancier second homes.

About 85 out of 100 Finns live in **urban** areas. Helsinki is both the nation's capital and its biggest city. More than 1.3 million people call it home. People in Finnish cities usually live in multistory apartment buildings. Stand-alone homes are more common in the countryside. They are **traditionally** made of wood. Many homes and apartments across Finland have **saunas**. Workplaces often have them, too.

Whether in cities or **rural** areas, most families own at least one car. People often use public buses, trams, and **ferries** to get around large cities. Finns also take planes to travel over the nation's rough **terrain**.

TRAM

CUSTOMS

People in Finland celebrate a variety of art forms. Sculptures are often modern and displayed in settings from city parks to forests. Finland is known around the world for its design tradition. Marimekko **textiles** are bright and used in clothes and home goods. The nation is home to celebrated glass and **ceramic** artists.

SCULPTURE PARK OF
VEIJO RÖNKKÖNEN

SÁMI CLOTHING

It is common for Sámi people to wear their traditional clothing, known as *gákti*. Both men and women wear brightly colored pullovers. They may be decorated with reindeer fur and leather. The gákti also includes fur boots with curved toes.

Music is woven into Finnish **culture**. Theater and opera performances are enjoyed year-round. Some Finnish folk music tells stories about the country. It is often played with a stringed instrument called the kantele. Heavy metal music is hugely popular in Finland. Helsinki hosts the Tuska Open Air Metal Festival each summer.

17

Children in Finland start school the year they turn 7. Basic education includes grades one through nine. Students take classes in Finnish, math, environmental studies, art, and sports. They start learning foreign languages, geography, history, and science by fifth grade. At age 16, some students attend a **vocational** school. Others attend general secondary school. Students who pass an exam may go to university.

About three out of four Finns have **service jobs**. Some have jobs in hospitals, hotels, or banks. Others are highly trained teachers in Finnish schools. Factories in Finland produce electronics, cars, and paper products. Farmers grow oats, wheat, potatoes, and sugar beets.

HARVESTING SUGAR BEETS

CLEVER CREATIONS

Finns invented ice skates, the sauna, the rescue toboggan, and the first wireless heart rate monitor. The world has a Finnish inventor to thank for the video game *Angry Birds*, too!

HELSINKI

SAUNA

Many Finns love to spend time outside. The activities they choose vary by season. In winter, people snowshoe or cross-country ski. Ice skating and ice hockey are also common pastimes. Most Finns use a sauna at least every week. Some jump in snow or cold lakes to cool down.

CROSS-COUNTRY SKIING

In warmer weather, people in Finland often boat, swim, or fish. Older Finns may Nordic walk using special poles that help with balance and upper body exercise. Mushroom and berry picking are popular traditions. Common indoor activities include dancing and going to concerts.

NORDIC WALKING

MAKE A *HIMMELI*

Himmeli are small Christmas ornaments. Finns traditionally make them from reeds or straw. You can use drinking straws instead.

What You Need:
- a ruler
- string
- scissors
- 4 drinking straws

What You Do:
1. Measure and cut a 3-foot (0.9-meter) piece of string.
2. Cut each straw into three equal pieces.
3. Start by threading three straw pieces onto your string. Move the pieces into a triangle shape.
4. Tie a knot so that your triangle keeps its shape. You should have a very short "tail" at the end of the triangle and a long "tail" with the rest of the string.
5. Thread two more straw pieces onto the long piece of string. This forms a second triangle. Tie another knot to keep it in place.
6. Repeat Step 5 until you just have a single straw piece left over.
7. Thread your final straw piece onto the string. Tie the string that is left over onto the short "tail" created in Step 4.
8. Pull together the last two triangles. Use another piece of string to tie them together. Display the himmeli in your home!

21

ROBERT'S COFFEE

COFFEE CRAZY!

Finns love their coffee. An average Finn uses more than 20 pounds (9 kilograms) per year! By law, workers in Finland get two coffee breaks each day.

Different kinds of porridge are typical breakfasts in Finland. People make the whipped porridge *vispipuuro* with semolina, milk, and fresh fruit such as red currants. Another popular breakfast or lunch is Karelian pies. Inside their rye pastry crust is rice porridge with egg butter on top.

22

Perunarieska is a favorite Finnish food. This potato flatbread is usually served with butter or smoked salmon. Finns often fry reindeer meat and serve it with mashed potatoes and lingonberries. Schools, restaurants, and some workplaces commonly offer pea soup for lunch every Thursday. Thin pancakes with jam are served alongside the soup.

KARELIAN PIES

PERUNARIESKA

FINNISH PANCAKES

Make this simple dish for breakfast or a snack. It is quick to cook! Have an adult help you prepare it.

Ingredients:
2 cups whole or 2% milk
2 eggs
1/4 cup melted butter
3/4 cup flour
1/2 teaspoon salt
canola oil or butter for the pan
fresh berries or jam

Steps:
1. Pour the milk and eggs into a large bowl. Whisk them together, then add in the butter.

2. Add the flour and salt into the milk mixture. Blend with a hand mixer or whisk until the batter is smooth. Let the batter sit for 30 minutes.

3. Lightly oil a large frying pan or griddle over medium-high heat. Drop about 1/4 cup of the batter onto the pan and cook for about 2 to 3 minutes, until the bottom is golden brown.

4. Flip the pancake over and cook for another 2 to 3 minutes so both sides are golden brown.

5. Repeat Steps 3 and 4 until you run out of batter.

6. Serve with fresh berries or jam. Enjoy!

23

On Palm Sunday or Easter Saturday, young Finns may dress up as witches. They bring decorated willow twigs and offer blessings to neighbors. In exchange, the children receive candy or coins. Growing grass in pots or on plates is another Easter tradition.

EASTER

SANTA AND SAUNAS

On Christmas Eve, many Finns visit the graves of family members. Families also relax in the sauna on this night. Santa Claus, known as *Joulupukki*, brings presents to well-behaved Finnish children.

Midsummer is a major holiday for Finns in late June. They celebrate warm weather and the Midnight Sun with barbecues and bonfires. On December 6, Finns celebrate Independence Day. People often have fancy dinners. They place blue and white candles in their windowsills to honor the country. Throughout the year, people in Finland come together to enjoy their culture and traditions.

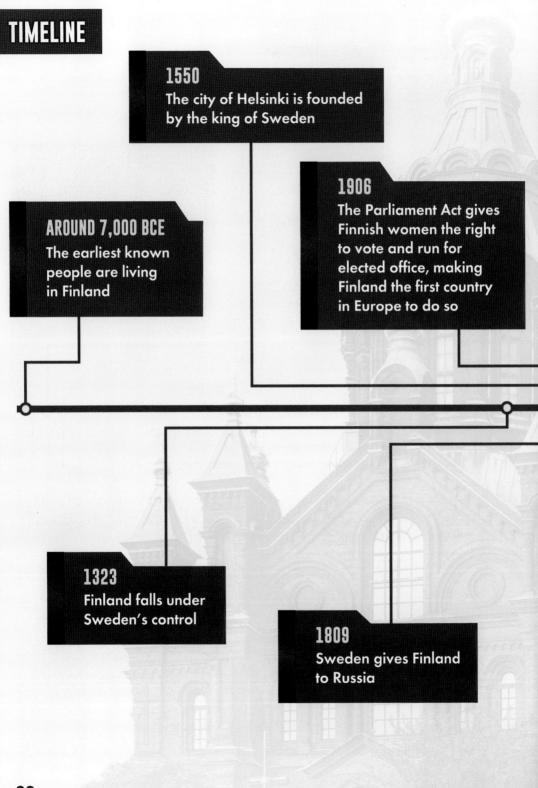

1550
The city of Helsinki is founded by the king of Sweden

1906
The Parliament Act gives Finnish women the right to vote and run for elected office, making Finland the first country in Europe to do so

AROUND 7,000 BCE
The earliest known people are living in Finland

1323
Finland falls under Sweden's control

1809
Sweden gives Finland to Russia

2000
Tarja Halonen is elected as Finland's first female president

2019
Finland's government promises to be carbon neutral by 2035

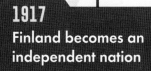

1917
Finland becomes an independent nation

1995
Finland amends its constitution to recognize the Sámi as Indigenous people and guarantee stronger rights for them

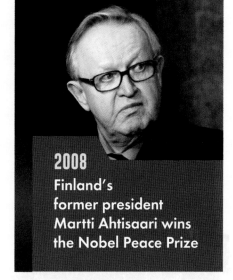

2008
Finland's former president Martti Ahtisaari wins the Nobel Peace Prize

FINLAND FACTS

Official Name: Republic of Finland

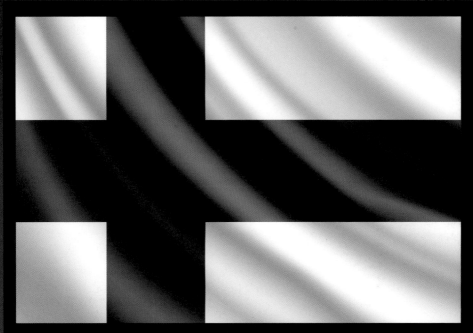

Flag of Finland: The flag of Finland is white with a horizontal blue cross. This cross is found on the flags of the other Nordic nations. The blue stands for the country's many lakes. The white represents the snow which blankets the land during wintertime. Finland adopted this flag design in 1918.

Area: 130,559 square miles (338,145 square kilometers)

Capital City: Helsinki

Important Cities: Tampere, Turku, Espoo

Population: 5,601,547 (2022 est.)

WHERE PEOPLE LIVE

COUNTRYSIDE
14.3%

CITY
85.7%

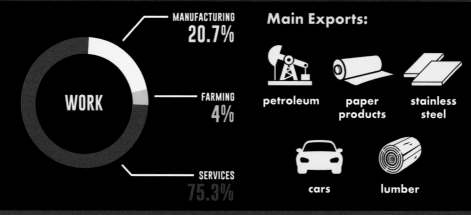

MANUFACTURING
20.7%

WORK

FARMING
4%

SERVICES
75.3%

Main Exports:

petroleum

paper products

stainless steel

cars

lumber

National Holiday:
Independence Day, December 6

Main Languages:
Finnish, Swedish (official languages)

Form of Government:
parliamentary republic

Title for Country Leaders:
prime minister (head of government), president (chief of state)

RELIGION

NONE
30.6%

OTHER
1.7%

GREEK ORTHODOX
1.1%

LUTHERAN
66.6%

Unit of Money:
euro

GLOSSARY

ancestors—relatives who lived long ago

Arctic Circle—an imaginary line that circles the top of the globe, parallel to the equator

ceramic—the material made when clay is hardened by heat

culture—the beliefs, arts, and ways of life in a place or society

deciduous trees—trees that lose their leaves every year

ferries—boats or ships that carry people and goods, typically on a regular schedule

graze—to eat grass or other plants that are growing in a field or pasture

gulf—part of an ocean or sea that extends into land

Indigenous—related to people originally from an area

Nordic—related to a group of nations in northern Europe that share similar cultures; the Nordic nations are Finland, Sweden, Norway, Denmark, and Iceland.

northern lights—colorful natural lights that appear in the sky; northern lights most commonly occur within or near the Arctic Circle.

rural—related to the countryside

saunas—small rooms used for hot-air or steam baths meant to clean and refresh the body

scavenge—to look for food that is already dead

service jobs—jobs that perform tasks for people or businesses

terrain—the surface features of an area of land

textiles—fabrics that are woven or knit

traditionally—according to customs, ideas, or beliefs handed down from one generation to the next

tundra—frozen, treeless land; beneath the surface, tundra is permafrost, or land that is permanently frozen.

urban—related to cities and city life

vocational—involved in the training of a skill or trade that prepares an individual for a career

TO LEARN MORE

AT THE LIBRARY

Gould, Sloane. *Finland*. New York, N.Y.: Cavendish Square Publishing, 2022.

McClanahan, Ben. *Northern Lights*. Lake Elmo, Minn.: Focus Readers, 2019.

Spanier, Kristine. *Finland*. Minneapolis, Minn.: Jump!, 2022.

ON THE WEB

Factsurfer.com gives you a safe, fun way to find more information.

1. Go to www.factsurfer.com.

2. Enter "Finland" into the search box and click 🔍.

3. Select your book cover to see a list of related content.

INDEX

The images in this book are reproduced through the courtesy of: Grisha Bruev, front cover, pp. 5 (Uspenski Cathedral), 19 (Helsinki); O.C Ritz, pp. 4-5; Alex Stemmers, p. 5 (Lake Saimaa); Jamo Images, p. 5 (Olavinlinna Castle); Karl Ander Adami/ Alamy, p. 5 (Salla National Park); Irina Sen, p. 8; nblx, p. 9; Misterlvad, p. 9 (Helsinki); photomaster, p. 10 (Eurasian lynx); Aliaksandr Mazurkevich, p. 10 (reindeer); Stanislav Duben, p. 10 (great gray owl); Peter Schwarz, p. 10 (moor frog); Erik Mandre, pp. 10-11; Nature/ Alamy, p. 12; Andy Martin Jr/ Alamy, p. 13 (Tuukka Rask); Alexander Chizhenok, p. 13 (Lappeenranta); MDowningUK, p. 14; Folio Images/ Alamy, p. 15; Evgeniy Egorov, p. 16; footageclips, p. 17; ullstein bild / Contributor/ Getty Images, p. 18; Nataliia Zhekova, p. 19 (harvesting); New Africa, p. 19 (ice skates); Frolphy, p. 20 (top); MinttuFin, p. 20 (bottom); Aleksandra Suzi, p. 21 (Nordic walking); burnel1, p. 21 (himmeli); Tina Zhou, p. 22; StockphotoVideo, p. 23 (top); Fanfo, p. 23 (middle); ElenaBoronina, p. 23 (bottom); BlueOrange Studio, p. 24; OLIVIER MORIN / Contributor/ Getty Images, p. 25; ZUMA Press, Inc./ Alamy, p. 27 (top); REUTERS/ Alamy, p. 27 (bottom); thodonal88, p. 29 (euro banknote); Andrey Lobachev, p. 29 (euro coins).